In the quiet of the evening
when the stillness of the night
silently creeps around, may you
find solace somewhere in
this little book, then slowly close
your eyes in sleep, and know that
God is all ways there

Love

Thoma

Reach Out and Touch

Reach Out and Touch

Perry Tanksley

FLEMING H. REVELL COMPANY
OLD TAPPAN, NEW JERSEY

Library of Congress Cataloging in Publication Data

Tanksley, Perry.
    Reach out and touch.

    1. Devotional literature. I. Title.
BV4832.2.T35   242   73-22344
ISBN 0-8007-0663-3

Jesus came over and touched them. "Get up," he said, "don't be afraid."

MATTHEW 17:7

The world was blessed when Jesus touched
A world that needed Him,
And now it needs Him just as much
But we must reach to them.
And we are part of Jesus' plans;
For healing He imparts
Is now dispensed through Christian hands
And comes from loving hearts.

I expect to pass through this world but once. Any good therefore that I can do, or any kindness that I can show to any fellow creature, let me do it now. Let me not defer or neglect it, for I shall not pass this way again.

STEPHEN GRELLET

For the whole Law can be summed up in this one command: "Love others as you love yourself. Love them one by one.

GALATIANS 5:16

LOVE THEM ONE BY ONE

I tried to love the world
But didn't succeed as such.
I tried to love a continent
But Africa was too much.
I tried to love Americans—
Two hundred million great,
But I lacked love enough
To even love my state.
I had not love enough
To throw my arms around
Twenty thousand people
Here in my own hometown.
Distressed, I cried in shame,
"Lord Christ, who loves the world
Teach me to learn to love
And serve as You have served."
He said, "Try it one by one—
Neighbors, family, friends;
Love people you work with;
They're part of a world to win.
Love servants who serve you
And greet each boy and girl.
Get interested in people
In your corner of the world.
Indeed God loved the world
And gave His only Son!
But you can't love that many
So love them one by one."

Nobody will know what you mean by saying that "God is love" unless you act it as well.

LAWRENCE PEARSALL JACKS

**Your strong love for each other will prove to the world
that you are my disciples.**

JOHN 13:35

Our love is so limited that we can hardly imagine the love of God. It's vaster, stronger, and more enduring than we can grasp. It is an active love, emanating from the cross of suffering and the empty tomb. So great a love must be sent through a person. It first came through Jesus Christ. Now it comes through people like us. As the Word was made flesh when Jesus came, so now it must be made flesh through Christians.

Lord, if Thy written Word
Should need an explanation,
Then let Thy Word in us
Experience incarnation.
That Christ the Living Word,
Once robed in flesh of men,
May live in us and prove
Thy Word's made flesh again.

Instead, be kind to each other, tenderhearted, forgiving one another, just as God has forgiven you because you belong to Christ.

EPHESIANS 4:32

TO BE CALLED PEACEMAKER

Each effort to be kind
With Christlike open-mindness
Returns huge dividends
That prove the worth of kindness.
And in a world gone mad
We more and more will find
Greatness is still measured
In terms of being kind.
And still the best compliment
That one can hope for here
Is to be called *Peacemaker*
By friend and foe and peer.
Then in the spirit of kindness
Amidst earth's strife-cursed factions
Let us be kind and prove
Greatness in words and actions.

If the sum of our unspoken admiration, love, approval and encouragement could find expression, nine-tenths of the world's woes would be healed as if by magic.

MARGERY WILSON

8

When a man is trying to please God, God makes even his worst enemies to be at peace with him.

PROVERBS 16:7

Jesus said, "Blessed are the peacemakers, for they shall be called [children] of God" (Matthew 5:9 RSV). Please notice that the outsiders, the unreached, the unsaved may not know us as children of God until they see us as peacemakers. The implied suggestion is that those same people may not acknowledge we are children of God if we are troublemakers or indifferent about making peace. Since that is true of the non-Christian, it is doubly true of fellow Christians. A Christian has an inner knowledge that his task is to be a peacemaker. Even though he may fall short at times, the Christian has a right to expect every other Christian to be a peacemaker. A peacemaker is one of God's best witnesses. A troublemaker serves Satan.

> If there were no churches to attend
> And you couldn't tell it at all
> That you loved Jesus Christ—
> Then what would you be called?
> If you were a peacemaker
> And Christlike amidst strife,
> They'd know without your saying it
> That you loved and served Christ.

No, he has told you what he wants, and this is all it is: *to be fair and just and merciful, and to walk humbly with your God.*

MICAH 6:8

TRUEST GRATITUDE

One proves his gratitude
To those for whom he cares
With loving deeds much more
Than loving words he shares.
For truest gratitude
To friends true-blue to you
Can only be expressed
By kindly deeds you do.
And sweetest spoken words
Cannot compare, indeed,
With acts of love performed
When someone stands in need.
It's not that words don't count
But gratitude in fact
Takes up where speech leaves off—
Performing grateful acts.

Thank God every morning when you get up that you have something to do that day which must be done whether you like it or not. Being forced to work and forced to do your best, will breed in you temperance and self-control, diligence and strength of will, cheerfulness and content, and a hundred virtues which the idle never know.

CHARLES KINGSLEY

And in the same way—by our faith—the Holy Spirit helps us with our daily problems and in our praying. For we don't even know what we should pray for, nor how to pray as we should; but the Holy Spirit prays for us with such feeling that it cannot be expressed in words.

One of the gifts of the Holy Spirit seldom remembered is *helps*. The average Bible student is unaware that a special gift of helping is promised as a result of being full of the Spirit. Too many of us prefer the gift of prophecy or evangelism or teaching. There seems to be greater acclaim for men behind podiums or pulpits. Yet there is desperate need for Christians with the gift of *helps*. Barnabas probably had that gift for the name the church bestowed upon him was Son of Consolation. Andrew was not noted for evangelistic preaching, but he is pictured in the Scripture as a helper. The Bible is full of notable people whose talents were large, but it is balanced with many lesser people who made the most of helping others. If you can help others in the Name of Jesus and with the spirit of love, you are His helper.

> She loved to help people
> Every chance she received,
> And witnessed with her life
> And with each helpful deed.
> Visiting, listening, sharing,
> She won some to Christ's side,
> And without her knowing it
> She influenced hundreds of lives.

11

After I have poured out my rains again, I will pour out my Spirit upon all of you! Your sons and daughters will prophesy; your old men will dream dreams, and your young men see visions.

JOEL 2:28

WHEN ONE IS SIXTY-NINE

Life has been so good,
I've much to give thanks for;
My heart is strong and gleeful,
My eyes see every star.
I would have been content
To merely survive,
But, Lord, You made it better—
What a thrill to be alive!
Fragrant springtime flowers—
The odor of fresh-plowed earth—
Pungent rain, warm sunshine—
Lord, it's like a new birth.
With neighbors to love
And children, dear Lord,
My life is a song
Without a discord.
The future holds no fear
Since without measure
My sixty-ninth birthday
Is a river of pleasure.
With days growing brighter,
I sense all future days
Will unfold revealing
My golden decade.

Our todays make our tomorrows, and our present lives determine the bridge on which we must enter the next life.

MINOT J. SAVAGE

**Every good thing the Lord had promised them came
true.**

                                                        JOSHUA 21:45

As long as you have breath in your nostrils, God has a plan for your
life. Then waste no more time reminiscing over the past or complain-
ing over the present or worrying over the future. God has a reason for
allowing you to survive. Believe that and you will do more than just
survive. Life will become a new adventure every day as you seek for
the purpose of God for your being here.

If God has a plan
Of indescribable beauty
For people like me,
Then I'm reporting for duty.
If every breath is planned
And each step of the way,
Then I'm reporting for duty
To find God's will today.

But among you it is quite different. Anyone wanting to be a leader among you must be your servant.

MATTHEW 20:26

GREATNESS MEANS GIVING

> Too long I measured life
> By gifts bestowed on me,
> Or else of fame I earned
> Or winning some degree.
> What fools that we should measure
> In terms of stored-up gold
> The greatness of a person
> By gifts on him bestowed.
> The measure of a life
> Is not in terms of pleasures
> Derived from fame you've earned
> Or owning rarest treasures.
> It has to do with treating
> Prodigals like brothers,
> And the giving of self
> In service to others.
> Try giving yourself away
> In unselfish living.
> Greatness is never getting,
> It's always giving.

Life is hardly respectable if it has no generous task, no duties or affections that constitute a necessity of existence. Every man's task is his life preserver.

RALPH WALDO EMERSON

**It is as the Scriptures say: "The godly man gives gener-
ously to the poor. His good deeds will be an honor to him
forever."**

2 CORINTHIANS 9:9

Shallow thinkers sometimes persuade us to accept stored-up wealth as the one key to greatness. Often we judge the greatness of a person by the number of servants he has. Jesus came with the true measuring rod of greatness. Not how much you store up determines greatness, but how much you give, suggested our Savior. He taught us to judge greatness not by the number of servants we have, but by the number of people we serve. Did He not say, "If you would be great you must be a servant of others" *(see* Matthew 20:26)? If Christ is our Savior and Master, then let Christians discard the popular measuring rod of greatness based on wealth obtained, or servants employed. Let us strive for the true greatness.

> He gave his wealth for missions
> And people mocked his act,
> And when he died he left
> Nothing at all, in fact.
> Much smarter than his heirs
> Who cursed his will that day,
> He stored his wealth in heaven
> By giving it away.

All of us must quickly carry out the tasks assigned us by the one who sent us, for there is little time left before the night falls and all work comes to an end.

DOING GOLDEN THINGS

Why don't I take the time
Of which God gives so much
And do those deeds which give
To time a golden touch?
Why must I fritter away
With inconsequential strife
The years God gives and miss
The higher use of life?
What if my life in quantity
Lacks the quality plus,
And yet I look and see
It's happening to all of us.
We know we've been alloted
So many days from birth
To bless a needy world
Or else to blight and curse.
I'll take the time God gives
To follow Jesus Christ
Assured I'll not regret
The use I've made of life.
Then let us all join hands
With time that's left to give
And do those golden things
That make friends glad we lived.

All the time which God allows us is just enough for work which God allots us.

ANONYMOUS

16

Another reason for right living is this: you know how late it is; time is running out. Wake up, for the coming of the Lord is nearer now than when we first believed.

The night is far gone, the day of his return will soon be here. So quit the evil deeds of darkness and put on the armor of right living, as we who live in the daylight should!

ROMANS 13:11-13

The memory of a misspent life, wasted time, unused talents, and hoarded treasures will be a part of the pangs of judgment. What if you awake in the afterlife and discover you have missed your destiny? What if too late I find out I violated the will of God and missed God's blueprint and failed in my purpose? Such an abrupt awakening would be a foretaste of damnation for me. Then ought we not attempt to use our lives in the service of our Lord and Master? To avoid the unending memory of a life misspent, we should more seriously consider obedience to the will of God.

> To seek God's will
> And then to turn it down
> Is to invite failure
> And to miss the crown.
> To consider God's will
> And do it in part,
> Saying no to one facet,
> Rebreaks Jesus' heart.

THE WORLD AWAITS BRIGHT MINDS

Now that you're graduating
And your diploma's earned,
You may be prone to think
You know all there's to learn.
But wide horizons beckon—
And truths that really matter
Invite your mastery
As you climb up the ladder.
Diplomas earned must never
Become the end of earning
New milestones of achievement;
You are not free from learning.
The world awaits bright minds
And too long has been waiting
Those who will go on learning
After graduating.

What we truly and earnestly aspire to be, that in some sense we are. The mere aspiration, by changing the frame of the mind, for the moment realizes itself.

ANNA JAMESON

> **For the man who uses well what he is given shall be given more, and he shall have abundance. But from the man who is unfaithful, even what little responsibility he has shall be taken from him.**
>
> MATTHEW 25:29

So long as there is one ignorant cell in your brain, you have a duty to make it literate. So long as one lobe of your brain needs teaching, you are indebted to see that it is properly taught. Our intelligence is a latent gift, a hidden talent, and so long as our minds are allowed to lie fallow, we sin against ourselves and against our God. Most of the ills of the world remain unsolved because individuals like you and me failed to educate our minds and apply our intelligence to problem-solving. This leads us to two other facts: In a sense, each person is responsible for his own education. Instead of blaming poor facilities or bad teachers, the honest person should admit he is his first and biggest hindrance. The other fact is simply that God wants our intelligence properly educated for problem-solving and people-helping purposes.

So long as people languish
And for the good life are yearning,
I must prepare myself to serve,
And so I'll go on learning.
As long as souls in darkness
Long for someone to come sharing
The Good News of our God,
Then I'll go on preparing.

19

I bless the holy name of God with all my heart. Yes, I will bless the Lord and not forget the glorious things he does for me.

PSALMS 103:1,2

LOOK WHAT I FOUND

In terms of selfish recompense,
My life made very little sense.
In terms of pleasures of the flesh,
My life was very dull at best.
In terms of hoarding precious gold,
My life was purposeless and cold.
In terms of craving fame and power,
My life, once fresh, grew stale and sour.
But I, until I found the Christ,
Knew not there was a better life.
In Christ one finds more than a creed.
I found a Friend who met my need.
I found a Comrade in my labor;
I found One dearer than my neighbor.
I found a Guide for unsure feet
Who led me through the vales of grief.
I found in Christ my heart's content
And everything in life makes sense.
All that I crave I've found in Christ:
Wealth and purpose—abundant life.

Too late I loved Thee, O Beauty of Ancient Days! Yet ever new! And, lo! Thou were with me and I abroad searching for Thee! Thou were with me, but I was not with Thee.

SAINT AUGUSTINE

SHALL I LOOK to the mountain gods for help? No! My help is from Jehovah who made the mountains! And the heavens too! He will never let me stumble, slip or fall. For he is always watching, never sleeping.

PSALMS 121:1-4

Life is a riddle and most people never solve the puzzle. Only One can interpret the meaning of your existence. That One created you to begin with and understands your deepest desires and strongest yearnings. God became like us; God entered human form; God dwelt in our midst that He might speak our language, interpret life's meaning, and solve the riddle of our existence. One wastes his time consulting other philosophers and teachers when Jesus Christ has the Words of life. Most try other answers only to be forced back to Him, who said, "I am the Way—yes, and the Truth and the Life" (John 14:6).

Everything I've ever craved
I've found in Christ my Master,
For He's the end of searching
For everything I'm after.
I sought in worldly pleasures
And searched each truth and creed
Only to discover Christ offers
Everything I seek and need.

A man they call Jesus made mud and smoothed it over my eyes and told me to go to the Pool of Siloam and wash off the mud. I did, and I can see!

JOHN 9:11

DOES IT WORK!

It's never wrong to inquire and ask
About a faith you cannot grasp,
And, since our God became a Man,
There are facts difficult to understand.
At least I found I could not grasp
Answers to certain questions I asked.
But I switch on lights without a query
About the complex electric theory.
I eat nor waste a single minute
On theory of vitamins, except trust in it.
The proof of a theory is does it work?
Understanding it may drive me berserk.
So if you've found forgiveness for sin
And if you were blind but see again,
And if, enslaved, you're now set free,
Then Christ works for you as He works for me.

Christian faith is a grand cathedral, with divinely pictured windows. Standing without, you see no glory, nor can imagine any, but standing within every ray of light reveals a harmony of unspeakable splendors.

NATHANIEL HAWTHORNE

Are there still some among you who hold that "only believing" is enough? Believing in one God? Well, remember that the demons believe this too—so strongly that they tremble in terror! Fool! When will you ever learn that "believing" is useless without doing what God wants you to? Faith that does not result in good deeds is not real faith.

JAMES 2:19,20

What practical people we are in all areas of life except one. We never ask, "How can a red cow eat green grass and give white milk and yellow butter?" We practical people drink milk without inquiry. We are not quite so practical when it comes to Christian faith. This is a faith to be tried and tested. If it works, apply it. If it doesn't, discard it. So the Scriptures suggest, "O taste and see that the Lord is good!" (Psalms 34:8 RSV). This is a faith to be experienced before it is understood. Some things the heart experiences which the mind cannot grasp. I enjoy some phases of television, but I don't understand how television works. When it comes to Christian faith, let us be at least that practical.

> Let agnostics question
> The reality of Christ;
> I know that He's real
> And lives in my life.
> Let sceptics denounce
> All things they cannot see;
> I've experienced the Presence
> And I know God loves me.

Your power and goodness, Lord, reach to the highest heavens. You have done such wonderful things. Where is there another God like you? You have let me sink down deep in desperate problems. But you will bring me back to life again, up from the depths of the earth. You will give me greater honor than before, and turn again and comfort me.

PSALMS 71:19-21

Of things that mean the most
And of things that mean much,
Certainly the most meaningful
Is when two lives touch.
For something very special
Which I cannot define
Happened to me personally
When your life touched mine.
Memories of that moment
Now cling without my clutching,
And life is good because
Our hearts and lives are touching.